The Date Deck

…'cause every couple needs a date night

Esther Boykin, LMFT

The information contained within this book is for informational and entertainment purposes only. It is not a clinical recommendation or diagnosis by any of the authors or their representatives. A qualified professional can only make specific recommendations for your unique relationship and/or mental health after one-on-one assessment.

www.grouptherapyassociates.com

Table of Contents

Preface

The evolution of this book has been a personal one for me. It started out as a guide to help some of the couples that I worked with in my couples therapy practice. So many of my clients were motivated to improve their relationship but found themselves too busy to make time for fun with each other. I pointed out that just a little creativity and forethought was all they needed to jump start their romance again but most still struggled.

So I decided to do some of the legwork for them. I compiled a deck of date night idea cards and sent them home. Most enjoyed the dates and some came back with their own ideas and variations of my suggestions. I was thrilled and inspired to share these ideas with even more couples. And so *The Date Deck* was born.

It didn't take me long to want to update the first edition of The Date Deck. I had more ideas to share and wanted to tweak some of the original date nights. But before I could begin to add new dates, I got a burst of inspiration from my husband.

On our way out to dinner with friends one night, he asked me, "What is your obsession with *date night*? Honestly it just seems like something on the 'therapist' to-do list' and not part of anyone's *real* life."

I'm going to be honest here- that did not feel like an inspirational moment at the time. In fact it felt a lot more like someone just burst my balloon. I was annoyed and he was sorry to hurt my feelings but unwilling to completely dismiss his question as meaningless.

It took me a while but eventually I put my hurt feelings aside and started to think about what he said. We've been married long enough for me to know that his intention was not to crush my excitement for date night or question my expertise. He had a valid question, why do couples experts like myself obsess about date night? I started to wonder just how many other people were thinking the same thing he was. How many people see books like this and say to themselves, "*who really does date night and more importantly what's the point?*"

His question was not about our date night (even if it felt like it was), it was about understanding the reasoning behind this so-called relationship rule that so many experts, books, and blogs tout as necessary to a happy relationship. He was really asking why I'm so invested in writing this book and encouraging couples to keep dating.

And while few husbands would dare ask those questions, especially not on date night, I appreciate that my husband did. He opened my eyes to a new perspective. Despite the research to support the importance of date night, few of us relationship experts really bother to tell couples *why* it matters. We offer ideas and encourage you to keep doing it but rarely do we take time to talk about the specific ways a date can improve and maintain your love for each other.

I believe when you understand how something can benefit you; you're significantly more motivated to actually follow through. Understanding the connection between your actions and the end result can shift your perspective. Suddenly what you *should* do becomes the thing you *want* to do.

And I want you to *want* to date each other. I want date night to be something that makes you excited and joyful about your relationship and the time you spend together.

So it is with that goal in mind that I re-wrote this book. I set out to offer not only date night ideas but also some understanding of how these dates can transform your relationship. I hope you find inspiration and insight on the following pages and most of all I hope you discover the joy of dating the one you're with!

~ *Esther*

Welcome to the Date Deck

Is Date Night Really That Important?

Relationship experts and happy couples agree that "dating" is crucial to the health of your relationship. Date night helps couples be intentional about their connection to each other and doing new and fun things keeps the romance and passion from fading away.

But all too often, life gets in the way.

Work, school, family, and friends- it's a wonder you find any time for each other at all!

And when you finally do, who has the energy to come up with a plan?!

That's where **The Date Deck** comes in.

In a review of relationship and marriage studies, researchers[1] have found that relationships benefit from date night in five major ways:

1. **Communication:** It creates opportunities for better communication, which is an essential part of a healthy relationship.

2. **Novelty:** The experience of doing new and exciting things together fosters intimacy and sustains your interest in each other.

3. **Romantic Love:** Date night rekindles the spark of romance and encourages couples to sustain those feelings over the long haul.

4. **Commitment:** Consistently making time for date night creates a sense of togetherness and demonstrates a couples' commitment to each other.

5. **De-Stress:** Date nights are meant to be fun and playful, the perfect antidote to stress, which can be detrimental to relationships.

In these pages you'll find creative date ideas that are couple-tested and therapist-approved to put the fun and romance back in your relationship.

Because every couple needs a date night!

[1] Wilcox, W. B. & Drew, J. (2012). The Date Night Opportunity: What does couple time tell us about the potential value of date night. Website: http://nationalmarriageproject.org/wp-content/uploads/2012/05/NMP-DateNight.pdf

How to Use This Book

This book is meant to serve as both an instruction manual and source of inspiration. The dates included have gotten the thumbs up from my test couples and offer you the chance to work on specific aspects of your relationship without even thinking about it.

Each section of the book offers dates to meet specific needs such as Quickies for when you are extra busy or Rekindling Romance when you feel like things have become distant between you.

The date descriptions include tips on how to make it happen as well as a note explaining why the date is good for your relationship. Dating should be fun but it's also a great way to "work" on maintaining (or repairing) your love.

I know that not every date idea in here is going to be a perfect fit for everyone but I hope that you'll let each one inspire you. Tweak them to fit your budget and your lifestyle. The goal is not to do each date exactly as written but rather to find your own creative variations to keep your relationship fresh and fun.

With that in mind I've also included a page for your own Date Night Review. Use the questions on these pages to make notes about what worked, what didn't, and whether or not you want to try this date again. This is a great opportunity to discover what you and your significant other enjoy most in a date. Remember, date night is not just fun; it's also a chance to learn more about each other.

Now get out there and start dating!

Quickies

No time for date night? No way! On the following
pages are perfect dates that you can fit in between
meetings, soccer games, and whatever other obligations
are crowding your calendar.

Don't let a lack of time keep you from enjoying some
fun with your sweetheart. You can squeeze most of
these dates into 30 minutes or less. While that may not
seem like a lot of time, I promise you that a short date is
always better than no date at all!

*"A great date is not determined by how much
time you spend but by how you make each
other feel with whatever time you've got."*

HAVE A BREAKFAST DATE

Great dates don't only happen in the dark. Start your day right with a good meal and even better company. You can head to the kitchen for a quick coffee and toast or to a favorite diner for something more substantial.

Starting the day together is a sure fire way to keep connected no matter how busy your schedule gets. And if you want to really show some extra attention, surprise them with a tray of goodies in bed before they wake up.

Why this date works…

One of the reasons that date night is so vital to a healthy relationship is that it ensures regular connection with your partner minus distractions. Stress and overwhelming schedules can quickly wreak havoc on even the most loving relationship but a few moments focused on each other at the start of a hectic day can actually reduce stress and shift your perspective.

Even if it's just 15 minutes over a cup of coffee, giving each other some undivided attention is a quick and easy way to promote good feelings all day long. And when you reduce stress at the start of the day, you increase the chances that your time together at night will be much happier.

Date Night Review

What did you like most about this date?

How did this date help or challenge your relationship?

Would you like to do to this again? Why or why not?

Date In Unexpected Places

Forget dinner reservations or concert tickets, book your next date night at your local grocery store. That's right, in the middle of your weekly grocery trip you can carve out some time for a date.

Many large chain stores such as Whole Foods and Wegmans, offer shoppers a variety of in-store restaurant options from sushi to salads to pizza. Not interested in what your local grocer has to offer? Get creative. Stop at the juice bar inside your gym or sneak off to the bakery next door to your dry cleaner for a mini-date escape.

Why this date works...

We all have errands to do and it's easy in a world of over-booked schedules and demanding jobs to let them eat up every free moment in your life. By building in some date time during these mundane weekly tasks you create a sense of fun in what would otherwise be a boring to-do list.

The bonus? If you plan to have a date night while grocery shopping or while your kid is at basketball practice then you both have to go. And it is truly in those small daily chores that you are reminded that you are building a life **together**.

Date Night Review

What did you like most about this date?

How did this date help or challenge your relationship?

Would you like to do to this again? Why or why not?

Have a Virtual Date

Maybe one of you travels a lot for work. Or maybe you work opposite schedules. Whatever the reason, at some point or another most couples have a phase where they just aren't in the same space long enough to date. Thank goodness for technology.

In this age of Skype and Facebook, smartphones and tablets- there's no excuse not to do date night, even if it's virtual. You can choose to flirt via text message all day long or set aside a little time in your day to close the door to your office or sneak away from your kids and video chat. You can even set up private social media accounts like Instagram or Twitter that you only share with each other. Just be careful how you send those *special* photos and messages so know one else can see.

Why this date works…

Technology can be a huge distraction and create distance for many couples but it also has the power to connect you to each other's daily lives like never before. One of the primary goals of date night is to make time to share the parts of your life that don't include each other.

By creating virtual dates you can give each other a window into your time apart. A loving relationship is about feeling seen and understood but couples often miss out on that because they're so busy living life apart. Virtual dates reconnect you to each other in ways that will make your time together even more meaningful. Understanding that your boyfriend had a terrible commute or that your wife's big presentation was a success, gives you an opportunity to support and encourage each other in real time which keeps you both feeling more connected.

Date Night Review

What did you like most about this date?

_____

_____

_____

_____

How did this date help or challenge your relationship?

_____

_____

_____

_____

Would you like to do to this again? Why or why not?

_____

_____

_____

Be Spontaneous

Sometimes the most time-consuming part of date night is the planning. So today, skip the debate about which restaurant or what time and just do it. Have you been dying to see that new movie? Grab your partner and just go. Cancel the dentist appointments or skip this month's PTO meeting and go do something fun instead. Skip the gym or the nail salon and clear the other distractions for a little while and remember sometimes the best dates are the ones that just happen.

Why this date works…

I remember when my children were in elementary school they implemented a program called D.E.A.R.- *Drop Everything And Read.* It was great, at various times during the school week, no matter what class the kids were in, they were required to stop what they were doing and read.

This new program sent the message that good reading skills were the top priority, even if most days they spent hours focused on other subjects. While I have no doubt that this intruded on teacher's instruction time for other subjects; ultimately it was an important lesson for everyone. To succeed we must always focus on the fundamentals.

That same principle applies to your relationship. Although you spend countless hours everyday focused on other people and other things, your significant other is still the top priority. It's easy to tend to the call of bosses, friends, and children while ignoring your partner's need to be loved but the cost can be high.

Just like those school children, in our relationships it's important to D.E.A.L {*Drop Everything And **Love***}. An unexpected lunch date or last minute plan to go to a concert are simple ways to remind each other that no matter how busy you get, your relationship is still the most important priority.

Date Night Review

What did you like most about this date?

How did this date help or challenge your relationship?

Would you like to do to this again? Why or why not?

Fun & Playful Dates

Far too often, couples that have been together for a while start to treat date night like just one more task on the weekly to-do list. Dating is meant to be fun, whether it's your first date or 500th!

These ideas are designed to help you tap into your creative and playful side. Adopt an attitude of silliness and really dive into these dates as a chance to reconnect with the carefree side of yourselves.

"Nurture your friendship... it's the foundation on which the rest of your relationship is built."

Have a Photo Shoot

Photos are about preserving memories and capturing the special moments in your life. That doesn't just mean the milestones - the daily moments of connection and the fun times you share deserve to be captured on film too!

Check your local mall or Google for photographers in your area and book a session. You don't have to buy all the photos but the experience will be fun.

If a professional photo shoot is out of your budget or seems too formal, just grab your camera or cell phone and have some fun being silly in front of the lens. Or better yet, turn it into an adventure by trying to find an old-school photo booth at a local boardwalk, arcade, or carnival.

Why this date works…

American author and photographer, Eudora Welty once said, "A good snapshot keeps a moment from running away."

Preserving moments is exactly why a photo shoot makes for a great date night idea. We live busy lives and even when you aren't inundated with things to do, our natural tendency in relationships is to become a little forgetful when it comes to the good stuff. It's easy to focus on what your partner does wrong or what's missing and equally easy to overlook all the wonderful and loving moments you share together. A photo shoot gives you more than just a fun experience; it gives you a tangible reminder of your love.

And if you really want to turn up the passion, try booking a boudoir photo session instead. While the thought of creating sexy pictures may make you a little anxious at first, the process of getting it done will be well worth the effort.

Date Night Review

What did you like most about this date?

_____

_____

_____

_____

_____

How did this date help or challenge your relationship?

_____

_____

_____

_____

Would you like to do to this again? Why or why not?

_____

_____

_____

GO TO A GAME

Even if one of you doesn't love sports, the energy of the crowd in the stands and the bliss of indulging in some stadium food can't be beat! Go ahead, cheer for the home team and enjoy the rush of adrenaline as you ride the waves of emotions with the crowd. Now take that passionate energy home with you and create your own winning moment!

Can't afford to see the pros? Check out your local minor league teams, same big fun with a much smaller price tag.

Why this date works...

Watching a live sporting event brings a unique energy to dating. A big part of the experience as a spectator is feeling connected to the team or athlete you're watching. We all have a friend or relative who is a huge sports fanatic. They dress in team colors. They know all the personal information about their favorite players. And they act as if they're an integral part of the team's success or failure even though there's no tangible connection between their life and that of the team.

While this may seem like a crazy way to behave when you aren't sharing in the million dollar pay check that players get, it is also a passionate example of how to be emotionally invested in someone else's success.

Every individual has their own hobbies, projects, or goals that don't include their partner. Maybe one of you is starting a business, or training for a marathon, or is just passionate about your college football team. No matter the individual passion, our desire to have the person we love invest *emotionally* in our success or failure, even when the outcome doesn't impact their life in any tangible way, is universal.

Sharing in the experience of rooting for complete strangers to win a game that will have zero effect on your daily life is a powerful way to connect with each other. Shared passion, whether it's for a sports team or for one person's personal goal, is one of the fundamental aspects of a loving commitment.

Date Night Review

What did you like most about this date?

How did this date help or challenge your relationship?

Would you like to do to this again? Why or why not?

DO SOMETHING ARTISTIC

This is not a test of your artistic abilities so don't panic if your idea of a portrait is little more than a stick figure. Instead look at this date as a chance to be free and creative together.

Nearly every town across the country has a paint-your-own-pottery shop or an art school offering weekend workshops or mini-classes you can join. Another really fun option that's popping up in lots of major cities, are art studios that cater to date night outings. They offer inexpensive open studio hours usually with food, drinks, and all the art supplies included. And best of all they clean up the mess when you're done!

Don't overlook the DIY options. Just hit your local arts and crafts store to pick up whatever supplies interest you and go crazy. Have kids? It's ok to turn it into a family date night and let everyone get in on the action.

Why this date works...

The arts are about making your own rules - trying new colors, shaping clay into something unique, taking raw materials and turning them into something beautifully original. It's a lot like love.

It's also one the most expressive forms of communication. Therapists use art all the time to help clients, young and old, articulate their feelings without words. However it takes a certain amount of vulnerability to express yourself through art, especially as an adult with less than impressive artistic skills.

An artistic date night requires you each to take a leap of faith and be vulnerable with each other. As you look at each other's work, find ways to encourage and support the creative process. Ask thoughtful questions and remember that there are no wrong answers in art- whatever is expressed is perfectly beautiful.

The bonus? You just might uncover some hidden talents and create something you want to display in your home on a permanent basis. And if you're looking for a sexy upgrade to this date- try body paints and a large canvas. You can even find a kit online from companies such as Love is Art, designed to help you create your own unique paintings.

Date Night Review

What did you like most about this date?

How did this date help or challenge your relationship?

Would you like to do to this again? Why or why not?

Date Like Teenagers

Somehow, despite the lack of money, transportation, and privacy, dating when you're young is fun and exciting! Tonight skip the grown-up ideas of romance and focus on having fun like you did as a teen.

Go for a walk holding hands, share an ice cream or cuddle on the couch and enjoy the fact that you don't have worry about your parents coming in and spoiling the fun.

Don't know how to date like a teenager? Ask some teens or young adults what they do when they go out and try it. You may be surprised just how much fun you can have.

Why this date works…

As the parent of teenagers, I am amazed at what counts as dating these days. Sitting on the couch watching silly YouTube videos, hanging out with friends, listening to music, or going ice skating- all dates and all fun. The joy of being new to the world of dating is that there are no rules other than have fun and enjoy each other's company.

When you embrace this mindset of dating the pressure to do it "right" or plan the "perfect" date disappears.

Rather than focusing on *what* you're going to do together, you can focus on just *being* together. And when you let go of the desire to "get it right", you will find date night far more relaxing and enjoyable for both of you.

Date Night Review

What did you like most about this date?

....

....

....

....

How did this date help or challenge your relationship?

....

....

....

....

Would you like to do to this again? Why or why not?

....

....

....

Rekindling Romance

This book is focused on keeping the good vibes going in your relationship but what happens when things aren't going so well? One of the most common but rarely mentioned, reasons that couples aren't having date night is that they just aren't feeling the love in their relationship anymore.

We often envision date night as an expression of a happy relationship but it can also be a tool to reconnect and repair minor relationship hiccups. The dates in this section are designed to help you bring back a sense of romance and foster a closer emotional connection to each other.

"Real romance is rarely found in the grand gestures, but rather in the small details that say, 'you matter to me'."

STAY IN BED

Whether you have to skip your morning run or weasel out of brunch with the in-laws, find a day to linger in bed with each other. The lazy indulgence of just lounging together doing nothings is a great catalyst for conversation and cuddling- two critical components of a great date.

It's also the perfect opportunity to spark a little physical intimacy if you are both in the mood. But remember, the most important part of this goal is to just relax and enjoy doing nothing together, even if just for a little while.

Why this date works…

There are two key elements of this date that can have major impact on your relationship- tuning in to each other and physical touch.

When you're in bed for the purpose of date night, it's not the time to check your email or get on Twitter. This is a time to pretend the outside world doesn't exist and just focus on each other. This uninterrupted attention increases the intimacy between you almost instantaneously, which helps you both feel more connected.

And while you're in bed there should always be some snuggling and touching. I'm not suggesting sex or even foreplay with the goal of getting to sex (although those are certainly fun ways to spend your time in bed). For this date, start by focusing on just being close.

Everyone loves to be touched gently and affectionately by his or her partner. In fact, we are biologically wired for touch to be a vital part of our most important relationships. This date gives you the opportunity to practice using touch as a way to initiate emotional intimacy, not just sex. By using touch as an intimate connection you will rekindle the feelings that drive romance and ultimately give your relationship the boost it needs.

Date Night Review

What did you like most about this date?

_____

_____

_____

_____

How did this date help or challenge your relationship?

_____

_____

_____

_____

Would you like to do to this again? Why or why not?

_____

_____

_____

_____

GET (OR GIVE) A COUPLES MASSAGE

It's hard to think of a better way to get in the mood for love and romance than a nice long, relaxing rub-down. And when you can share it with each other, that's even better.

Call your local day spa and book a room for two or ask about couples massage lessons. Many places offer couples a chance to not only enjoy a massage together but also learn how to use those relaxation techniques at home with each other.

Why this date works...

We've already talked about the power of physical touch which is the obvious benefit of this date night but it's not the only reason a couples massage is a great date. When the love tank in your relationship is running low, it can be hard to ask for what you need in a way that is loving and encourages your partner to be responsive.

In order to fully enjoy a massage you have to practice asking for what you like and pay attention to your body's needs. These are skills that can be easily transferred to other areas of your relationship that require you to be honest and vulnerable.

And because it is an expected part of the massage process, you may find it easier to practice asking for what you like. Once you get comfortable, try using those same communication skills when it's time to talk about sex or other sensitive topics of conversation at home.

Date Night Review

What did you like most about this date?

How did this date help or challenge your relationship?

Would you like to do to this again? Why or why not?

Go For a Ride

The feel of the wind in your hair, the freedom of the open road, and {most importantly} the simple joy of just being in each other's company all make motorcycles a great date night idea.

When you go out for a ride there's no talking - just time to be together and express yourself through touch, so be sure to hold on tight.

No motorcycle? No problem. Rent one or try driving in a convertible or on a tandem bicycle instead.

Why this date works...

You've probably already noticed a theme in this section- lots of touch and a little less talk. Communication is an important part of rekindling the good feelings in your relationship but it can also be difficult when you are experiencing any kind of conflict or distance.

By focusing on being physically close and using touch to express your feelings of trust and love, you can more easily break down the defense mechanisms that may be making verbal communication hard. After your ride, try to talk about what it feels like to just be together in silence. Can you rediscover that feeling of comfort and closeness without words? I bet after this date you can.

Date Night Review

What did you like most about this date?

How did this date help or challenge your relationship?

Would you like to do to this again? Why or why not?

TAKE A COOKING CLASS

Eating can be a sensual and extremely sensory experience, making it perfect for couples looking to turn up the heat in their relationship.

Stores that specialize in kitchen and cooking products, like William-Sonoma or Sur La Table, often offer free or low-cost cooking classes. You can also try locally owned restaurants and in many areas there are stores dedicated to teaching the everyday cook some new tricks.

If you can't find one in your area, create your own class. Bring the laptop into the kitchen and dive into one of the fabulous food blogs or YouTube channels out there and get cooking.

Why this date works…

Whether you're foodie with a refined pallet or think of food as nothing more than fuel for your body, cooking is an act of love. Your body requires nourishment, and being thoughtful about the flavors and health benefits of the food you share with each other is also a powerful metaphor for the other ways in which you nourish your relationship.

Although it's easy to see cooking as just another chore, learning a new recipe or technique together can turn a mundane task into an opportunity for romance and nurturing. Date night is meant to help you focus on each other and using something as basic as cooking to create a shared experience allows you to bring connection back into your daily life.

Date Night Review

What did you like most about this date?

How did this date help or challenge your relationship?

Would you like to do to this again? Why or why not?

Budget Friendly Dates

One of the most common excuses I hear from couples is that they simply can't afford to do regular date nights. But it's just that... an excuse.

Date night doesn't require a significant investment of money in order to strengthen your relationship or bring joy into your daily life. In fact some of the best dates are free. Don't believe me? Check out the suggestions on the next few pages.

Special Note:

While this section includes dates that are specifically designed to be low-cost, nearly every date in this book can be done within your budget. I strongly encourage you to get creative and do as many dates as possible without breaking the bank.

"The secret to an amazing date isn't money or location, it's time and effort."

GET PHYSICAL

Exercise is an incredible {and free} way to improve your health, mood, and relationship. Sign up for a class at your local gym, pop in a DVD, or turn on a fitness-based video game and get those bodies moving.

If you're more of the outdoor kind of couple, exercise can be an amazing way to turn date night into a consistent habit. A daily walk or bike ride, or a weekend hike are all excellent ways to have fun together.

Bonus: Research shows that it's easier to stay on track with your fitness goals when you have a workout buddy.

Why this date works...

Far too often we associate exercise with some ideal body type or fad diet from a magazine. But the truth is that regular exercise is one of the most important ways you can take care of yourself. It helps your mood and reduces the risk of countless illness- whether you achieve those six-pack abs or not.

Exercise is self-care and making your significant other a part of your self-care routine can have a powerful effect on both of you. It sends the unspoken message that you care about each other's health and it makes a strenuous activity much more fun.

And best of all, the endorphins that are released post-workout are likely lead to another kind of physical activity too! *wink*wink*

Date Night Review

What did you like most about this date?

_____

_____

_____

_____

_____

How did this date help or challenge your relationship?

_____

_____

_____

_____

Would you like to do to this again? Why or why not?

_____

_____

_____

Have an Adventure

Travel is a fantastic way to create adventure in your life but you don't have to go to a new city or spend a fortune on a fancy resort to have a new experience together. It only takes a little creativity and effort to find the adventures in your own backyard!

Check out a travel guide, Yelp, or another resource to find out about new and hidden treasures in your city and then go explore.

Like to be a little more spontaneous? Get a new take on your neighborhood by pretending to be from out of town. The shift in perspective just might help you see your local attractions and each other in a brand new light.

Why this date works...

As much as we enjoy the comfort of the familiar, human beings are hard-wired to seek out novelty. Our brains are excited by new experiences and new places, in fact it's part of the reason you were so infatuated with each other in the beginning.

Like a kid with a new toy, we are enchanted with new love because there's so much to discover. And just like that kid, we can also become bored and quickly forget just how much fun it is to play together.

Thankfully you can recapture that feeling again in simple ways, like doing something new or unexpected in a familiar place. By creating new experiences with one another you will begin to see each other as fresh and exciting again. And just think of all the fabulous new stories you'll have tell!

Date Night Review

What did you like most about this date?

....

....

....

....

How did this date help or challenge your relationship?

....

....

....

....

Would you like to do to this again? Why or why not?

....

....

....

HAVE A FIRESIDE PICNIC

Humans have been gathering around the fire since we figured out how to light one and for good reason. The warmth and coziness of a fire is the perfect setting to share stories about your day and thoughts about your future.

It's also the perfect place for s'mores!

No fireplace? No problem. Recreate the romantic fireside glow with candles or venture outside with a fire pit or bonfire in the backyard.

Why this date works...

Watch any romantic comedy or read a romance novel and you'll find that firelight is sexy. Maybe it's the warmth of the flames or the way flattering glow that makes everyone look just a little more attractive. Whatever the reasons, we are drawn to fire. And because there is such a strong association for most people between fire and passion, it is one of the best ways to create a romantic date without breaking the bank.

Whether you have the ability to enjoy a fireplace, a bonfire, or just a couple of candles in your bedroom-use our primal fascination with flame to your advantage. Create an environment that naturally evokes a sense of romance to ensure a date night that really works.

Date Night Review

What did you like most about this date?

_____

_____

_____

_____

How did this date help or challenge your relationship?

_____

_____

_____

_____

Would you like to do to this again? Why or why not?

_____

_____

_____

Play a Game

Whether it's chess, checkers, or basketball; playing games is fun. Pull out a deck of cards or those old board games that are collecting dust in the closet and play something together.

Not into board games? Visit a toy store or bookstore to see if you can discover something new and interesting or go high-tech and turn on the X-box or PS4. And if the weather is nice, get outside and play tag or flag football instead

Just be sure to choose a game you both enjoy and try not to let your competitive spirits overshadow the fun.

Why this date works...

Somewhere on the road from childhood to adulthood most of us stop thinking of play as being important. In fact, most adults treat play as if it were something to be earned or a distraction from the "important work" of life. But that's the wrong attitude.

Play is a crucial part of a healthy life *and* relationship. It encourages you to be mindful and focus on the moment. It reduces stress and increases laughter and compassion. It refines your ability to compromise and share. And it nurtures creativity in problem solving. In short, it makes all of us better partners!

Playing together, no matter what games you like, doesn't just help you to develop your relationship skills, it also helps you to enjoy life a little together a little bit more.

Date Night Review

What did you like most about this date?

How did this date help or challenge your relationship?

Would you like to do to this again? Why or why not?

Special Occasions

Whether it's genuinely a special occasion or you're just in the mood to do something special, these ideas are about getting passionate and doing something a little indulgent together. While some of the ideas will require a little extra money, others just require you to invest some extra time and special attention. Either way, each date is a chance to put the sexy back in your relationship!

"Every day you are in love is a special occasion; make it count."

GET OUT OF TOWN

If date night is a challenge, then a weekend getaway may seem like mission impossible. But you *can* make it happen.

Whether your budget can handle a week in the tropics, a weekend camping in the woods, or just a night at the local hotel, the important thing is to change your environment.

Try travel sites that specialize in flash sales and last minute deals, like Jetsetter, Expedia, or Groupon Getaways. Or make it a truly adventurous time and just get in the car and drive till you find somewhere that interests you.

Why this date works...

Even if you don't notice it, your environment has a powerful impact on your mood. A messy office can lead to a sense of chaos and stress at work. The pile of laundry in your bedroom actually creates restless sleep patterns. So when you really want to put the spark in your date night, escaping the day-to-day environment can be the perfect solution.

It allows you to temporarily forget about your responsibilities and the mundane tasks of daily life.

You can be calm, relaxed, and present with one another in a way that doesn't happen at home.

Vacation date nights, whether for a day or a week, give couples the opportunity to just be with each other without pressure. When you don't have to get home to a babysitter or even think about making your bed or what to eat for breakfast, you suddenly have the space to think about what you enjoy appreciate about each other and your life together.

Date Night Review

What did you like most about this date?

How did this date help or challenge your relationship?

Would you like to do to this again? Why or why not?

CREATE A FANTASY DATE

Always wanted to drive a racecar? Secretly wish you were a celebrity being chauffeured around town to the hottest nightspots? Do you ever imagine yourself as a seductress hitting on that attractive man at the bar? Well stop dreaming and start living out those fantasies-with each other.

Rent a limo and book a private room at the best restaurant in town or meet each other at a local bar and pretend to be meeting for the first time. Whatever your fantasy is, you can create it in real life with a little effort and creativity.

And if you need a little help, look for an "experience" gift service provider like Cloud 9 Living, who will do all the legwork for you.

Why this date works...

When you explore your fantasies together you have a unique opportunity to see each other in new and intriguing ways. Fantasies are about embracing parts of ourselves that we typically keep hidden from the rest of the world. So sharing these thoughts with your partner is one way to increase the intimacy in your relationship.

Fantasy dates give you an opportunity to explore untapped or unexpressed parts of yourself in a safe and supportive way. It adds a sense of freshness and adventure that keeps you both engaged and curious about each other no matter how long you've been together.

Date Night Review

What did you like most about this date?

....

....

....

....

How did this date help or challenge your relationship?

....

....

....

Would you like to do to this again? Why or why not?

....

....

....

Host Your Own Awards Show

Celebrities do it. Athletes do it. Even politicians and humanitarians do it.

They give each other awards because they realize that in order to maintain excellence you have to make a point of acknowledging it. So whether you are in love with the "best kisser" or the "fastest kitchen cleaner"- give them an award!

It can be as simple as leaving them a little note card or as elaborate as a full on award night with trophies. However you do it, thank your partner for the things you love most. You never know, they just might thank you in their acceptance speech.

Why this date works...

If there is one thing that most couples don't do enough of it's show appreciation for each other. All the small things that your partner does that make your life easier or make you feel loved deserve to be recognized. It's easy to stop noticing these details in the midst of daily life and so when you do stop to say thank you, it pays to do it in a big way. Whether you do this publicly or privately, making a grand gesture of acknowledging the things you love and appreciate most about each other is important to the health of your love life.

Appreciation and gratitude are the foundation for positivity and friendship. You need to take time to recognize that the seemingly small acts of kindness and connection, are in fact gifts of love that help keep your relationship going.

Date Night Review

What did you like most about this date?

How did this date help or challenge your relationship?

Would you like to do to this again? Why or why not?

BE NOSTALGIC

While I firmly believe that couples are happiest when they can focus on living in the present, there are times when a trip down memory lane is just what you need. A date night centered on celebrating the big (and little) moments of joy you've experienced during your time together can be fun and romantic.

There are many ways to get nostalgic on date night. Celebrating an anniversary or a birthday? Recreate a favorite or memorable celebration from the past to celebrate the milestone.

You could also create a scrapbook commemorating your favorite moments or have one special picture framed. Or you can keep it simple and just spend some time talking with each other about your favorite times together.

Why this date works...

As your relationship grows, it is natural to become lost in the daily to-do list and trying to plan for the future. But when was the last time you really thought about how you got here? You probably remember those warm feelings of love (and lust). I don't doubt your ability to reminisce about your favorite moments together. But what typically fades is our ability to remember the details. You may remember how fun your girlfriend used to be but you probably don't think much about all the things you did to make her life easier. Or maybe you can count all the ways your husband was so romantic but what did you do to make him feel so special that he wanted to shower you with romance?

By planning a nostalgic date you force yourself to not only remember your good times, but also to do the small things that created those memories in the first place. The magic of a loving relationship is in the details that often get lost over time in the flow of daily life. Nostalgic date nights don't just bring back memories; they bring back the actions that create fond memories. It is those actions that will keep your relationship on track today and for years to come.

Date Night Review

What did you like most about this date?

_____

_____

_____

_____

_____

How did this date help or challenge your relationship?

_____

_____

_____

_____

Would you like to do to this again? Why or why not?

_____

_____

_____

The Essential Dates

There are just some dates that every couple should be doing on a regular basis. These essentials are tried and true, "classic" dates and they offer something special in their simplicity. While you are unlikely to find a date idea in this section that you've never tried before, I hope you will find a new perspective on them.

Pay careful attention to why these dates work and although it may seem unnecessary, I want you to make sure that you review them using the *Date Night Review* journal pages. You may be surprised what new things you discover about each other and your relationship when you do.

"A simple date can be extraordinary; the real magic lies in the details."

DINNER AND A MOVIE

Some might say it's a tired, old cliché but it doesn't have to be. Dinner and a movie can be a creative and cozy date night if you put in a little effort.

Mix things up by having a picnic at an outdoor film festival or bring a TV or laptop into the kitchen and watch a rental while you cook together.

Whatever you do, don't underestimate the charm of this classic date scenario, especially when you add your own creative twist.

Why this date works…

The simplicity of dinner and a movie can quickly lead to a boring date night routine but it's simplicity is also the thing that makes this an essential date for every couple. Simple can be monotonous but more importantly it can be comforting and serve as a blank canvas for your individual preferences.

When you're feeling too tired to plan an adventure or be creative, you can still have a good date by sharing a meal and show. Sharing a meal encourages regular communication and that's the foundation of your relationship. You can make this a time for familiar comforts like your favorite meal and a good old movie or add some creativity with a quirky new documentary or eating at the new restaurant in town. Either way this old tradition is like the little black dress of dates- it's simple and classic and when you don't know what to do, it's always a perfect fit.

Date Night Review

What did you like most about this date?

How did this date help or challenge your relationship?

Would you like to do to this again? Why or why not?

GO ON A FIRST DATE (AGAIN)

Remember the excitement of going on a first date? The nervous butterflies and the extra time you spent getting ready? You don't have to give all of that up for the sake of a long-term, monogamous relationship. Just ask your significant other out on a new *first* date.

Whether your plans include romance at home or an adventure out on the town, take time to make sure you're feeling {and looking} your best. Give it the same level of attention that you would if you had never met before.

First dates are all about making a good impression and *showing* your interest in the other person so go all in on this date.

As you plan each detail, ask yourselves, "If this were our first date, would they say yes to a second date?" If the answer isn't yes, you aren't trying hard enough.

Why this date works...

This date is especially important the longer you've been together. It's so easy to fall into a routine where date night is just something to check off the to-do list, instead of treating each date like a special event. Let me be clear, having a routine is not always a bad thing. In fact it often helps couples be consistent with date night. An there is a certain joy in having a familiar and comfortable routine with the person you love. But you still need the spark and excitement of a first date every now and then.

The real genius of having **another** first date is that you get to put your knowledge of each other to good use. Unlike most first dates where you are guessing at what the other person will like, you can now rely on your history together to demonstrate your love for each other in special ways.

First dates are also a great time to check in with yourself. Are you making time to get your hair cut or your nails done or even shave your legs? Taking care of your appearance is important to the health of your relationship. Not only does self-care make you happier, but it also lets your partner see the sexy, confident, side of you that they fell in love with.

Date Night Review

What did you like most about this date?

How did this date help or challenge your relationship?

Would you like to do to this again? Why or why not?

LEARN SOMETHING NEW

Take a class, visit a museum, share a book, take a
personality test- however you choose to do it, find a
way to learn something new together on a regular basis.

Each of you will continue to grow and learn as
individuals. But as you do, it's crucial that you also
find ways to grow together. Many of the other date
night ideas in this book can be your inspiration for
learning but don't stop there.

The next time you just can't decide what to do for date
night, ask your partner to name one thing they've
wanted to learn more about and then go do that. You'll
both be better for the experience.

Why this date works...

One of the challenges to really listening and acting on
our loved one's thoughts and feelings is that often as
relationships grow we begin to assume that we know
what they want, think, and feel even better than they
do. You may plan things without asking them or not
ask their opinion because you're confident you already
know what they think.

Over time in a close relationship, if you're paying
attention, you will know what your partner is thinking
or feeling a lot of the time. It is one of the nice things
about being in a relationship- feeling known and

understood. But this belief that you know *everything* there is to know about your partner can lead you to ignore the fact that they're growing and changing all the time.

Preferences, goals, thoughts and feelings about life change as time goes by. It's up to each partner to make it a priority to continue to learn new things about each other.

Be curious about who your significant other is and who they are becoming. Making learning and curiosity a constant part of your date night routine, is an easy way to ensure that you are continuing to develop as a team.

Date Night Review

What did you like most about this date?

How did this date help or challenge your relationship?

Would you like to do to this again? Why or why not?

DANCE LIKE NO ONE'S WATCHING

Few things can make a couple feel closer or more connected than dancing. It's expressive and fun and, depending on your skills, really hilarious. If you're like me and lack a certain amount of natural rhythm, don't worry. This is *not* a dance contest; it's a date.

Dance studios offer lessons in everything from the foxtrot to salsa dancing. But dance doesn't have to mean lessons or spending lots of money. Check your community for dance clubs and local restaurants offering live music. Of course you can always just turn on your favorite music at home too.

It doesn't matter if you decide to take ballroom dancing lessons, hit the local night club, or are twerking in your living room with the stereo cranked up- just grab your partner and get your groove on!

Why this date works...

Dancing is an excellent date activity because it combines the adrenaline rush of physical activity with the creative expression of the arts. It's a chance to get close and just do what feels good together without worrying about what it looks like.

The real secret to a long-lasting love affair is the ability to be vulnerable with and offer loving acceptance of our partner. Dancing together may seem like such a simple activity but in the process of selecting the music, moving your body, and figuring out how to get in sync with each other, you are practicing the kind of give and take that makes your relationship work.

Date Night Review

What did you like most about this date?

How did this date help or challenge your relationship?

Would you like to do to this again? Why or why not?

Create Your Own Dates

If there is one universal lesson I've learned in my 10+ years as a couples therapist, it's that every couple has their own "right" way to do things. On the following pages are blank spaces for you to create your own perfect date night ideas. Maybe they will be variations on some of the ideas I've laid out in this book or things you've done before and want to do again. Whatever you come up with, take some time to think about why these dates work for you and how they keep your love strong.

Happy Dating....

Date Night Idea

What should we do tonight?

_____

_____

_____

_____

_____

Why this date works...

_____

_____

_____

_____

_____

_____

_____

Date Night Review

What did you like most about this date?

How did this date help or challenge your relationship?

Would you like to do to this again? Why or why not?

Date Night Idea

What should we do tonight?

_____

_____

_____

_____

_____

Why this date works...

_____

_____

_____

_____

_____

_____

Date Night Review

What did you like most about this date?

_____

_____

_____

_____

How did this date help or challenge your relationship?

_____

_____

_____

_____

Would you like to do to this again? Why or why not?

_____

_____

_____

Date Night Idea

What should we do tonight?

Why this date works...

Date Night Review

What did you like most about this date?

_____

_____

_____

_____

How did this date help or challenge your relationship?

_____

_____

_____

Would you like to do to this again? Why or why not?

_____

_____

_____

Acknowledgements

Marcus and Tasha, thank you for being my reminder that date night still matters to "real" couples. Keep getting it in anyway you can; and don't forget to invite us when it's double date night.

Ben, thanks for always asking me the hard questions; even if I don't always like it. Your support allows me to follow my passion and live my purpose. And after 20 years together you still give me butterflies on date night.

Dominic and Emily, everything I do is about building a foundation for you to grow from. Thanks for trying to be patient when I'm writing and never being afraid to tell me when it's lame.

Llouana, thanks for holding down the fort and encouraging me to finally get this done. That's how we do it at GTA, and I'm so thankful for that.

About the Author

Esther Boykin, LMFT is a licensed marriage and family therapist and relationship advocate who is passionate about helping people build healthier and happier relationships. She believes that meaningful emotional connections start by knowing and loving yourself.

She is co-founder and CEO of Group Therapy Associates, a counseling and coaching agency in Northern Virginia. Esther is dedicated to helping people build authentic and lasting relationships through counseling, coaching, and classes.

Through her writing and her work at Group Therapy Associates, she creates new ways to make mental health, relationship skills, and personal growth accessible and enjoyable.

She offers couples and individuals a variety of ways to work with her to reach their goals including, traditional therapy, relationship classes, and coaching services. To learn more about her work visit the Group Therapy Associates website, www.GroupTherapyAssociates.com or find her on Twitter (@estherbmft).

Looking for more date night ideas and relationship tips?

Visit us online to get free access to our monthly online webcasts where our experts answer your most important relationship questions.

www.grouptherapyassociates.com/datedeck

29075847R00081

Made in the USA
San Bernardino, CA
13 January 2016